Off the Church Wall

Rob Portlock

INTERVARSITY PRESS
DOWNERS GROVE, ILLINOIS 60515

To Mom and Dad

©1987 by Rob Portlock

InterVarsity Press is the book-publishing division of InterVarsity Christian Fellowship, a student movement active on campus at hundreds of universities, colleges and schools of nursing. For information about local and regional activities, write Public Relations Dept., InterVarsity Christian Fellowship, 6400 Schroeder Rd., P.O. Box 7895, Madison, WI 53707-7895.

Distributed in Canada through InterVarsity Press, 860 Denison St., Unit 3, Markham, Ontario L3R 4H1, Canada.

ISBN 0-87784-753-3

Printed in the United States of America

Library of Congress Cataloging in Publication Data

Portlock, Rob.
   Off the church wall.

   1. Christian life—Caricatures and cartoons.   2. American wit and humor, Pictorial.   I. Title.
BV4517.P67   1987   277.3'082'0207   87-2774
ISBN 0-87784-753-3

17	16	15	14	13	12	11	10	9	8	7	6	5	4	3	2	1
99	98	97	96	95	94	93	92	91	90	89	88	87				

Introduction

I'm a twin. When my brother and I were born, I had my foot in his mouth. I guess that's how this business of humor and cartoons got started.

My first memory of drawing was at the kitchen table with my mother; she was showing me how to draw a toy soldier. After that, I drew all the time. Fred Flintstone and Murphy the Surfer were characters making daily appearances on the back of my schoolwork. As the years went by this doodling turned into a passion for drawing, and later into a vocation as an editorial cartoonist.

About five years after becoming a Christian, I decided to branch out beyond editorial cartoons and try my hand at cartoons about the church and about the Christian life. I began submitting them to Christian magazines around the country and, lo and behold, they were accepted.

And so I now submit these cartoons, many of which have been previously published in magazines, in hopes that you will enjoy where God has led me.

Rob Portlock

"It's come to my attention that there's been a minor split in the church."

"Remember the good ol' days when we'd just give 'em a Gospel of John?"

"Honey, why in the world do you feel unimportant?"

"We're in need of a volunteer."

"So I say, 'Honey, no pastor should go five years without a vacation,' and he says, 'Vacation, who needs a vacation?' "

"Row six, third left."

"Hi Jonah! I've been waiting for you!"

"We couldn't afford new choir robes."

"Farnsley! Is that any way for an assistant pastor to ask for a raise?"

"The Pastor's been reading about the rapture again."

"That was the best sermon on giving I've ever heard."

It's Thursday and St. Peter takes a break to watch "Cosby."

"Of course, feel free anytime to let me know what you think of the job I'm doing as your pastor."

"This may set an ugly precedent for future board decisions."

"I see you've had assistant pastor experience before."

"Remember, when your father comes in, we all yell 'Ring around the collar, ring around the collar!'"

"No Mr. Wilson, when I said God wants a sacrifice, I didn't mean your wife!"

"I didn't realize our Disneyland outreach would be this successful!"

"Now make like Samson!"

"And guess who we ran into on our Holy Land trip . . ."

Ark animals playing a joke on Noah minutes before launch

"It says, then finally the pastor's wife went bonkers."

"Just exactly where was your church camp this year?"

"He hits a golf ball like he preaches—long, to the left, and always near a hazard."

"Well, the pastor said to make myself at home."

"Smoking or nonsmoking?"

"Repeat after me, I will not make fun of my wife's cooking in my sermons!"

"And do you Ann take Arnold to be your husband, to have and to hold, love and cherish, until things get a littl
tough, you get burned-out, and split?"

"And now, with the state of affairs in our Youth Program, Pastor Jim . . ."

"They say it's a tough church to preach at."

"And I know I need not mention which team this congregation will be praying for in the upcoming season."

"There's a representative from the women's group here that wants to talk to you about your position on the woman's role in the church."

"I put down the wrong order number.
We just received 2,000 beanbag chairs!"

"No, no! I wanted a *heavenly* angel!"

Turning point of the youth weekend retreat.

"Let's paint the monastery red."

THE FIRST IRA

"I'm very happy to be your new pastor. Now, I'd like to introduce my wife."

"Go tell the ushers, Mrs. Perkins is playing Bob Dylan again!"

"Look! Our youth group! In our church!!"

"He was traded to Valley Church for a music director and a youth pastor."

"I know what I told you is just between us."

"What makes you think I need a vacation?"

"What's with the crazy hat?"

"Looks like the pastor's lost control of his congregation."

"My sermon today is titled: 'Once upon a time there was a big church that didn't tithe ten per cent. It looked like they'd have to move and rent. And the pastor got real bent.' "

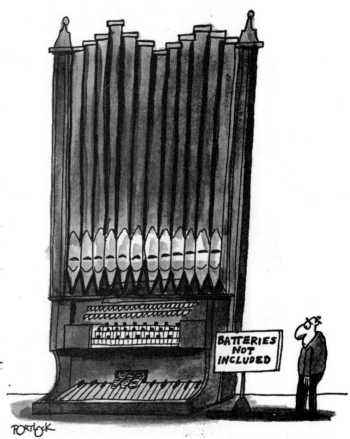

BATTERIES NOT INCLUDED

PORTLOCK

"I think it's time we do a little more background study on our new youth pastor!"

"It's what the pastor does to relax."

"I forgot to make the church mortgage payment last month."

"I'm here to tell you the board voted 8-0 for you to drop this Miami Vice trip!"

"Chester was just sure Christian Hubcaps would sell!"

"That's the last time I give my opinion on rock music!"

"My wife is under the weather today and couldn't come, but she sent her smile."

"I suppose it was too much to just come and have a picnic."

"He patterns his preaching after the Wizard of Oz."

"It happens whenever the pastor asks for volunteers."

"How can any normal, rational, intelligent, human being believe we came from that?"

Study aids

"Will the ushers come forward."

"In his will he said he wanted to be frozen until somone can see if his name's in the Book of Life; if it's not, leave him frozen."

"Can Pastor Rick come out to play?"

"You said you wanted to see a big prophet from the church fund-raiser!"

"Pastor, with this new version, instead of 10% tithing you can get 12½%!"

"I think this sanctuary movement thing is getting out of hand!"

"This isn't what I had in mind when I suggested that we make some money for the youth group."

"I take it the pastor's wife has heard all his sermons before."

"We're the church welcoming committee! We just dropped by to meet you!"

"So you thought you'd get away from the church for a day, huh? Don't you feel guilty? What about all your parishioners? And you call yourself a pastor . . ."

"Is it just me, or are his sermons getting longer?"

"O.K., on three, everybody roar and let's give Daniel a start."

Sermon practice

"I think we should have asked his price before he got here!"

"I don't know about you but I'm getting tired of some of these evangelists' methods of getting money!"

"You can always tell when he needs a vacation."

"I hate sitting behind the Johnsons!"

"And what am I supposed to make for dinner, Smarty Pants?"

"Welcome!"

"You and your bright idea to send the pastor to Disneyland on vacation."

"Hello sports fans . . ."

"He's changed my life. He communicates with me every day of the week. Anywhere I go he's there. He lets me know how I should live, what I should think. He tells me the true meaning of life. I just love Phil Donahue!"

"There's always a doubter in the crowd!"

"They donated it, but they didn't care for the offertory today."